SUITCASE BEAR ADVENTURES™

SEBASTIAN AT THE TOWER OF LONDON

By M.C. Hall

Illustrated by David T. Wenzel

bear&
company™

Published by Bear & Company Publications
Copyright © 2002 by Bear & Company

Printed in the United States of America

Suitcase Bear Adventures™ is a registered trademark of Bear & Company.

Based on a series concept by Dawn Jones
Edited by Dawn Jones
Designed by Valerie Hodgson

Library of Congress Cataloging-in-Publication Data

Hall, Margaret, 1947-
Sebastian at the Tower of London / written by M.C. Hall ;
illustrations by David T. Wenzel.
p. cm. – (Suitcase bear adventures)
Summary: On a visit to London with his human family, a teddy bear
decides to rescue the ravens imprisoned at the Tower of London by their
clipped wings, but instead learns a lesson in freedom and belonging.
ISBN 0-9713174-1-0 (alk. paper)
[1. Teddy bears–Fiction. 2. Ravens–Fiction. 3. Tower of London
(London, England)–Fiction. 4. London (England)–Fiction.] I. Wenzel,
David T., 1950- ill. II. Jones, Dawn L., 1963- III. Title. IV. Series.
PZ7.H14625 Se 2001
[Fic]–dc21
2001005170

To Alison and her childhood bears

M. C. *Hall*

Message to Parents

Bear & Company,

part of The Boyds Collection, Ltd. family,

is committed to creating quality reading and play

experiences that inspire kids to learn, imagine, and explore

the world around them. Working together with

experienced children's authors, illustrators, and educators,

we promise to create stories and products that are respectful

to your children and that will earn your respect in turn.

Table of Contents

Chapter One
London!

Sebastian pressed his nose against the rain-streaked window. "I'm glad I brought a raincoat," he said.

"Me, too," said Emily Parker.

"We told you it rained a lot in London," added Emily's little brother, Ben.

Sebastian, Emily, and Ben had arrived in London that afternoon. Now they were getting settled in at a lovely guest house.

Sebastian turned away from the window to look at the room. Flowered wallpaper covered the walls. There were two four-poster beds for Emily and Ben.

"Where will Ms. Valentine sleep?" Sebastian asked.

"Right next door," Emily answered. "And Mom and Dad are across the hall."

Mr. and Mrs. Parker traveled a lot, but they didn't like to leave their children at home. So Arabella Valentine came along as nanny and teacher for nine-year-old Emily and seven-year-old Ben.

Ms. Valentine wasn't in charge of Sebastian, however. Emily and Ben were. That was because Sebastian was a bear—a stuffed bear. Most people didn't realize that he was real—at least to the Parker children.

A moment later, the door opened and Ms. Valentine entered. She was tall and thin, with frizzy, red hair and bright blue eyes that didn't miss a thing. Drops of rain still clung to her curls.

"Are you unpacked, children?" she asked.

"Almost," said Ben. "Can we go sightseeing today?"

"I hadn't scheduled anything," answered Ms. Valentine. "I thought you would be tired after our long trip."

"Please," said Emily. "We don't have to meet Mom and Dad for dinner until 6 o'clock."

London!

"Where will Ms. Valentine sleep?" Sebastian asked.

Sebastian wondered what Ms. Valentine would say. She liked things to go according to schedule.

"Well . . ." Ms. Valentine pulled a small notebook from her shoulder bag. She flipped pages. "Certainly not the British Museum," she murmured. "And we need a whole day for the Tower of London. Picadilly Circus is a possibility, I suppose."

She closed the notebook. "Let me think about this while I get my raincoat," she said. "Meanwhile, finish unpacking."

Before the door closed behind Ms. Valentine, Sebastian was jumping up and down. "Picadilly Circus!" he cried. "Let's go there!"

"It's not the kind of circus with animals and acrobats," said Emily.

"What other kind of circus is there?"

"That's what Londoners call a place where a bunch of streets come together," Ben explained.

"Oh," said Sebastian in disappointment.

While the children finished unpacking, Sebastian pressed his nose against the window again. It seemed as if the rain was letting up, but he couldn't really tell. He climbed down and walked around, humming to himself. It was exciting to be in another country.

He liked looking at the taxis, the double-decker buses, and all the cars driving on the wrong side of the street. What he didn't like were the clothes. He tugged on his tie. It was too tight. But Emily had told him he looked very English.

"Cheerio, old chap," he said softly, trying out some words he had heard on an English television show. He had no idea what they meant.

The door opened again. "Are you done?" Ms. Valentine asked.

"Yes," said Emily.

"Can we go now?" Ben asked.

"*May* we, Benjamin," Ms. Valentine corrected. "And the answer is yes. We're off to Trafalgar Square to see a statue of a British hero."

"That doesn't sound exciting," said Sebastian as Emily settled him into her backpack.

"Shhh," said Emily gently. "Ms. Valentine might hear you."

"I doubt it," Sebastian sighed." She doesn't listen to me."

Chapter Two
Pigeon Food

Outside, the rain had become a light mist. "The weather has improved, so we don't need a taxi," Ms. Valentine said. "We'll take the Underground instead. That will be educational."

She folded her umbrella and marched off down the sidewalk. The children hurried to keep up.

"Are we going into a cave?" Sebastian asked.

"No," Emily answered. "The Underground is London's subway."

"They also call it the Tube," Ben added.

"Oh," said Sebastian, thinking that English

didn't sound the same in England.

"Here we are," announced Ms. Valentine. She pointed to a red-and-blue sign that said **UNDERGROUND**.

They went down some stairs, and Ms. Valentine bought tickets for Emily, Ben, and herself. *Bears get to ride free*, thought Sebastian with satisfaction.

A loud rumble announced the train's arrival. "Hold on to one another!" shouted Ms. Valentine as the crowd moved forward.

Once they were settled, Sebastian stared out the train window. There wasn't much to see. He was glad when the ride was over and they were back in the daylight.

"There is Trafalgar Square," said Ms. Valentine, pointing across the street. "Come along, now."

She guided the children to the square, watching for cars, buses, and bicycles. Then she led them to a fountain at the middle of the square. A tall column soared above. Sebastian leaned back, trying to see the top.

"This is Nelson's Column," announced Ms. Valentine. "Lord Horatio Nelson was an officer in the British navy. He died in battle in a place called Trafalgar in Spain. The column was built to honor him."

"Why are there lions at the bottom?" Ben asked.

Lions! thought Sebastian. *Lions in the city?* He didn't like that idea. "I don't hear any roaring," he whispered.

"They're statues, silly," said Emily. "Here, I'll put you down so you can see." She took off her backpack and helped Sebastian get out.

"Hey! Look at all the birds!" shouted Ben.

"Pigeons!" sniffed Ms. Valentine. "Filthy birds."

"People are feeding them," said Ben. "Can we? I mean, *may* we?"

"Yes, please," added Emily.

"I'm not sure that's a good idea," Ms. Valentine began. Then she looked at the children's eager faces. "Well, feeding pigeons is a tradition here. So I suppose you should have the experience. Just don't touch the dirty things."

"We won't!" Emily promised as she grabbed Sebastian. She and Ben hurried through the crowd to a man who was selling birdseed.

"We'd like two packets, please," Emily said politely.

"I like tradition, too," said Sebastian.

"Make that three packets," said Emily.

"That will be 60 pence, miss," said the vendor.

Pence were kind of like pennies, Emily remembered, but worth more.

"Come on, Emily!" cried Ben.

"No need to move, lad," said the vendor. "The birds will come to you." He was right. A flock of pigeons was already headed their way.

Emily handed a packet to Sebastian, then placed him on the ground beside her. She and Ben began to throw handfuls of seed into the air. Birds fluttered around them, cooing and pecking madly.

This is fun, Sebastian thought. He opened his birdseed. But a nearby pigeon startled him when it took off in a flurry of wings. Birdseed scattered everywhere.

Emily and Ben were too busy to notice. Quickly, Sebastian scooped up some seeds and threw them at the birds.

A few pigeons headed toward him, pecking away. One large bird raised its head. It eyed Sebastian greedily, then came closer.

"Go away!" cried Sebastian. "My birdseed is gone!"

But Sebastian was wrong. He had plenty of birdseed—all of it caught in his thick fur.

The pigeon pecked at Sebastian's head.

"Ouch! That hurts!" he cried.

Sebastian tried to shoo the pigeon away, but it ignored him. Soon it was joined by another bird, and then another.

"Help!" shouted Sebastian. "Help!"

At last, Emily heard his cries. "Leave him alone!" she shouted, dashing into the middle of the pecking pigeons.

"Emily!" called Ms. Valentine. "I told you not to touch those birds!"

"I'm not touching them," Emily called back. "They were hurting Sebastian!" She hugged her bear close. "You're safe now," she murmured.

Ms. Valentine hurried over. "Let me see," she said. "Goodness, he's covered with birdseed. And who knows what else. He's going to have to be washed and dried."

Sebastian shuddered. He remembered that when he had gotten into a jar of honey, Ms. Valentine put him in the washing machine. It had been awful.

"We'll give him a bath at the guest house,"
Ms. Valentine said.

Sebastian sighed. *It's better than the washing
machine*, he thought. *But not much.*

"Come along," said Ms. Valentine. "We need
to get back for dinner." She tucked Sebastian
under one arm and headed down the sidewalk.

Ms. Valentine is right, thought Sebastian.
Feeding pigeons isn't a good idea.

Chapter Three
The Changing of the Guard

"I missed you yesterday," said Sebastian. He had spent a long, lonely day draped over the shower rod, dripping into the tub.

"I missed you, too. But you're dry now, so you can come with us. And look, I cleaned your suit." Emily handed Sebastian his shirt, blazer, and tie—all neatly pressed.

The little bear sighed. He really didn't want to get all dressed up again. But he could tell it was important to Emily.

"I didn't get to see the museum," Sebastian said as he struggled with his buttons.

"Don't worry. We're going back this afternoon. It's too big to see in one day."

"Where are we going first?" Sebastian asked.

"To Buckingham Palace to see the Changing of the Guard."

"Are they changing their clothes?" Sebastian asked. "In front of people?"

"No," explained Emily patiently. "They change places. Some guards go home, and others come on duty."

"Oh," said Sebastian. That didn't sound too interesting. Still, it was better than hanging from the shower rod.

Once they reached the palace, Sebastian couldn't help being excited. The rain had ended, and the sun peeked out from behind the clouds. Crowds of cheerful people peered through the gates at the palace guards.

Sebastian studied the guards carefully. They stood stiffly, hardly seeming to breathe. "Are they stuffed?" he asked at last.

"No," said Emily. "They're alive. They just aren't supposed to move."

"I wouldn't like that," said Sebastian. He

always got wiggly after even just a few minutes of holding still.

Then they heard music. "Here come the new guards," said Ms. Valentine.

Emily and Ben pressed closer to the fence. At Emily's feet, Sebastian watched the guards move up the wide road. They were almost as stiff as the old ones. But at least they got to march.

The crowd pressed forward. The next thing he knew, Sebastian was through the bars and on the other side of the fence. *This is better*, he thought. *I can see everything.*

The music kept playing. Now the old guards started marching, too. They headed toward their replacements.

I can march, thought Sebastian. He lifted one foot, then the other. Head down, he moved forward. "1-2-3-4," he counted softly. "1-2-3-4."

On the last "4," Sebastian looked up. Both groups of guards were marching straight ahead, toward one another. And he was between them! He was going to be trampled!

"Sebastian! Watch out!"

Sebastian dashed back toward the fence. Emily's arm shot out and grabbed him.

"Sebastian," she said, "you could have been hurt!"

"I didn't mean to get in the way," said Sebastian. "I was just marching."

"I know," said Emily. "But you're not a palace guard."

"I'm a bear," Sebastian murmured, snuggling close. "Your bear."

"Well, children, that's it," said Ms. Valentine. "Now you can say you've seen the Changing of the Guard at Buckingham Palace."

"I'm glad she was too busy watching the guards to notice you," Emily whispered.

"And I'm glad you weren't," said Sebastian.

As they walked off, Ben asked, "Are we going to the museum now?"

"Yes," said Ms. Valentine. "But first I want you to see one of the best known symbols of London–Big Ben."

"Big Ben?" Ben repeated. "What's that?"

"It's a clock," said Emily. "Isn't that right, Ms. Valentine?"

"You're almost right, Emily. Many people call the clock Big Ben. But it's actually the name of the biggest bell in the clock tower."

Soon they could see the tower. "Wow," said Ben. "It's huge."

"Yes," Ms. Valentine agreed. "The second hand alone is 14 feet long."

"Cool. And it's named for me."

"It is not," said Emily. "It's older than you are. Maybe you were named for the clock."

"I was not."

"No arguing, children," said Ms. Valentine.

I'd like something to be named for me, thought

Sebastian. *A palace, maybe. Sebastian Palace sounds nice.*

"Now let's head for the museum," Ms. Valentine said. At her signal, a taxi pulled over. Soon they were on the way.

"We're going to see the mummies," Ms. Valentine announced.

"Is your mother at the museum, Emily?" whispered Sebastian.

"It's mummy—not mommy," Emily explained. "Mummies are bodies of Egyptians who lived a long, long time ago. They were wrapped up in strips of cloth before they were buried."

"Ugh. I don't think I like that kind of mummy."

"They'll be really interesting," Emily said. "Especially since we're going to Egypt soon."

Sebastian wasn't so sure about mummies being interesting. But once they reached the museum, he changed his mind. "These mummies were rich," he said as he looked around at all the treasures on display.

"They were kings," said Emily. "They had gold and jewels and all kinds of things buried with them."

Emily leaned over to study one of the exhibits.

Sebastian stood at her feet, staring at the mummy. Then he turned around—and jumped backward.

He was face-to-face with a crocodile!

"Sebastian!" cried Emily. She grabbed him just before he fell against a glass case. "Watch out! If you touch anything, you'll really be in trouble!"

"It's a crocodile!" Sebastian said, hiding his face against Emily.

"That's a mummy, too, silly. A crocodile mummy," Emily told him. "Now, you'd better behave. Or else Ms. Valentine will make me leave you in the room tomorrow."

"I'll be good," Sebastian promised. He stared at the crocodile.

It stared back with unblinking eyes.

Chapter Four
Touring the Tower

"There it is, children," Ms. Valentine said the next afternoon. "The Tower of London."

"There are lots of towers," said Emily. "I thought there was only one."

"I believe there are actually 20," said Ms. Valentine. "I'm sure we'll find out. Today is a perfect day to tour the Tower. There isn't a cloud in sight. Now, wait here while I get our tickets."

Sebastian wondered if Ms. Valentine had planned the weather, too. He decided that she probably had.

While they waited, the little bear looked over

Emily's shoulder. A great wall of stone stretched in all directions. Behind it, rooftops, windows, and towers with spiky spires poked into the sky.

"It looks like a castle," Sebastian said.

"Ms. Valentine said there *is* a castle inside," Emily replied. "The White Tower. It's the oldest castle in Europe."

"Does the queen live there?" asked Ben.

"No, Benjamin," said Ms. Valentine, who had returned with three tickets in her hand. "A long time ago, the rulers of England lived in the Tower. But now only the Yeoman Warders do."

"What are they?" asked Emily.

"Not 'what,' but 'who,'" said Ms. Valentine. She pointed to a man dressed in a dark-blue uniform and wide-brimmed hat. "That gentleman is a Yeoman Warder. The warders have guarded the Tower since it was built more than 900 years ago."

"He must be very old," whispered Sebastian.

Emily laughed. "It's not still the same man, silly bear."

"Oh," said Sebastian.

"Why does it say ER on his uniform?" Ben asked.

"E is for Elizabeth," Ms. Valentine explained,

"and R is for Regina, which means 'queen' in Latin."

She led the children to a tour group. As the group crossed a bridge, the warder explained that there had once been a moat underneath. But now there was no water—just grass.

"Directly ahead is the Bell Tower," the warder said. "At one time, the bell warned of attack. Now it rings every evening to tell visitors it is time to leave."

As the warder talked, Ms. Valentine reached into her shoulder bag. She pulled out her notebook and began to read.

At last, she snapped the notebook shut. "We're going to leave the group for a while, children," she announced. "We must see the Crown Jewels. There is always a line to get into the exhibit, so I want to do that first. We will rejoin the group afterward."

Ms. Valentine herded Emily and Ben across the green lawn toward a large building. A long line of people snaked out of the door.

"I don't like lines," said Sebastian.

"I don't like to wait, either," Ben agreed.

"No complaining, Benjamin," Ms. Valentine said sternly. "The Crown Jewels are an important piece of history. They are worth waiting for."

While they stood in line, Ms. Valentine talked about the jewels. Sebastian listened for a few minutes. But before long, he felt as if his head was getting too full. He wiggled.

"Can I get down?" Sebastian whispered.

Emily was listening to every word Ms. Valentine said. So she just nodded, took off her backpack, and helped Sebastian climb out. "Stay here," she whispered back.

The little bear looked around. From where he stood, there wasn't much to see but grass, cobblestones, and legs.

Then a movement caught his eye. It was a big, black bird. And it was staring right at him.

"Hi," said Sebastian nervously. He was glad he didn't have any birdseed in his fur this time.

The bird moved closer to him. "Hello, old chap," he said.

"Are you here to see the Crown Jewels?" Sebastian asked.

"Heavens, no," the bird replied. "I live here."

"Are you a king?" asked Sebastian.

"Well, no. Though I like to think of the raven as a kingly bird," said the bird. "That's what I am, a raven. My name is Thor."

"Oh," said Sebastian. "I'm a bear. My name is Sebastian."

"Pleased to meet you, Sebastian," said the raven. "Have you seen the Traitor's Gate yet?"

"No," Sebastian replied.

"Ah, you must," said Thor. He went on to explain that prisoners had entered the Tower through that gate. "And many never left alive," he added in a spooky voice.

Sebastian shivered. "That sounds scary," he said to the raven.

"It is," said Thor. "And that's not the scariest thing here. I've heard warders talk of a ghost that walks the Tower grounds at night. They say–"

He was interrupted by a loud squawk. "That's Odin," said Thor. "I must see what he wants. Good-bye." He fluttered his wings and walked off.

"Good-bye," called Sebastian, wondering what the warders had said. He turned and realized that he was staring at a strange pair of legs. Emily was lost! And that meant he was, too!

Chapter Five
Prisoners!

Sebastian hurried along the line of people, looking for Emily's striped socks. He had almost reached the door of the Jewel House before he spotted them. Emily was still listening to Ms. Valentine, who was still talking about the Crown Jewels.

Why, I don't think Emily knows we were lost, thought Sebastian. *So she probably hasn't been worried.* He was glad he had found her in time. He knew that looking for each other was not on Ms. Valentine's schedule.

A minute later, Emily bent to pick him up. "At

last!" she said. "It's our turn."

Inside the Jewel House, gold and jewels sparkled from glass cases. There were crowns and necklaces, swords and scepters, plates and cups.

"Look at this," said Ms. Valentine. "The diamond at the end of this scepter is one of the largest in the world."

The children moved closer to the display. From his place in Emily's arms, Sebastian leaned forward.

"Don't let your bear brush up against the case," warned Ms. Valentine. "An alarm might go off."

Sebastian pulled back his paw. He didn't want the guards to think he was a jewel thief. He could end up as a prisoner in the tower.

For almost an hour, they moved from one display to another. One crown started to look much like the next to Sebastian. He was bored.

"Are we almost done?" he finally asked Emily. "I want to see the scary stuff."

Ben overheard. "What scary stuff?" he asked.

"Gates and ghosts and things like that," Sebastian replied.

"Ghosts! Really?"

Ms. Valentine turned. "Emily," she said, "don't be scaring your little brother with nonsense about ghosts."

"I won't, Ms. Valentine," Emily sighed.

"I'm sorry," Sebastian whispered. "Usually she doesn't hear me."

"We're going on the Wall Walk now," Ms. Valentine announced.

Sebastian was quiet as Emily strapped him into her backpack. Walking on a wall sounded like fun. Though he couldn't imagine how they would do it. And he was surprised that it was Ms. Valentine

27

who had suggested such a thing.

She led the way up a steep staircase. When they reached the top, Sebastian suddenly understood. There was a wide, stone walkway running along the top of the wall.

"Wow! You can see everything from up here!" cried Ben.

"There's the Bell Tower," said Emily.

"And the Jewel House," Ben added.

Sebastian leaned over Emily's shoulder to see. It was a long way to the ground. He felt a little dizzy.

"I don't think bears are supposed to be up this high," he said in a shaky voice.

"Don't worry," said Emily. "I won't let you fall."

"I hope not," said Sebastian.

As Emily moved ahead, the little bear began to relax. He still held on tightly with one paw, but he was soon brave enough to look around.

The people below seemed very small. The treetops looked like giant green umbrellas spread over the crowds. Ahead of them, along the southern edge of the tower, the river gleamed like silver.

"I don't think bears are supposed to be up this high,"
he said in a shaky voice.

Before long, Sebastian decided that he liked being up high. As long as he was safe with Emily, of course. He was almost disappointed when it was time to go down.

On the ground again, Ms. Valentine looked around. "We can join that tour group over there," she announced. She led the way to a Yeoman Warder who had a crowd gathered around him.

Sebastian only half-listened to the guard, who was talking about kings and queens. The little bear was feeling a bit sleepy. He leaned his head against Emily and closed his eyes.

* * *

A raven's call woke Sebastian. He wasn't sure how long he had napped. They were still with the tour group, but they were now standing in a different spot.

Sebastian yawned widely. Then he realized the Yeoman Warder was talking about ravens.

"I met a raven," he whispered.

"Shhh," Emily said. "Listen."

"Of course, no one wants the ravens to leave the Tower," the warder was saying. "That's why their wings are clipped. A few feathers are removed so that the birds can't fly."

"Does it hurt?" someone asked.

"No," the warder answered. "It's like having your fingernails cut."

Sebastian remembered that he hadn't seen Thor fly. The bird had fluttered his wings and walked off. But Sebastian hadn't realized that Thor *couldn't* fly.

"And this ends our tour," the warder said next. "I hope you enjoyed your visit."

The crowd murmured, then began to move away. "It's time for us to leave, children," said Ms. Valentine. "We must rest before dinner. After all, this will be a late night. We're returning for the Ceremony of the Keys this evening."

As they left the Tower, Sebastian was thinking very hard. His thoughts weren't happy ones.

"It's awful," he murmured. "The ravens are prisoners in the Tower of London!"

He had to do something to help them.

Chapter Six
Sebastian's Mission

"Benjamin, please do not talk with your mouth full," Ms. Valentine said.

"I'm sorry," Ben mumbled. Bread crumbs fell from his mouth.

Ms. Valentine sighed. "This is exactly what I mean," she sighed. She began to explain how Ben could improve his table manners.

Sebastian, who was sitting on Emily's lap, decided that this was a good time to get Emily's attention. He hadn't had a chance since leaving the Tower. So now he tugged on her sleeve.

"I have to talk to you, Emily."

"What's wrong?" she asked. "You sound upset."

"I *am* upset," said Sebastian. "Isn't it terrible?"

"Isn't what terrible?"

"Clipping the ravens' wings so they can't fly."

"Oh," said Emily. "I don't think it's so bad, Sebastian. They have a nice home and plenty to eat. There's even a Yeoman Warder who takes care of them. He's called the Ravenmaster."

"But they're not free! Don't you think they should be?"

Miss Valentine finished with Ben and turned toward them. "Emily! Please sit up straight, dear."

Emily lifted her head and shifted in her seat.

Sebastian sighed. Shouldn't birds be able to fly wherever they wanted? Wasn't that what they were supposed to do? Wasn't that what it meant to be free?

"We must go now, children," said Ms. Valentine. "We have to get our tickets and raincoats. I want to be at the Tower before the ceremony starts."

An hour later, they were back at the Tower of London, which was dark and still at this hour. Emily and Ben were excited. It was unusual for

them to stay up so late. And it was exciting to be inside the Tower at night.

At exactly seven minutes before ten o'clock, the Chief Warder came into sight. He was wearing a long, red coat. In one hand, he carried a ring of keys. In the other, he held a lantern with a flickering candle inside.

The Chief Warder marched toward a group of other warders. Each guard saluted as he passed. One took the lantern from him. Then the Chief Warder moved from gate to gate, locking each in turn. When he'd finished, he marched back to his starting point. A sentry waited there.

The sentry called out, "Who comes there?"

"The Keys," replied the Chief Warder.

"Whose keys?" asked the sentry.

"Queen Elizabeth's Keys."

Sebastian was watching from a bench. Emily stood nearby. She was staring at the scene, her blue eyes shining in the lamplight.

Slowly and quietly, the little bear climbed off the bench. As his rear paws reached the stone walkway, he looked at Emily again. She hadn't noticed his movement. It was a good thing he had changed into his traveling clothes. The dark colors helped to hide him.

As Sebastian slipped away, he felt a little guilty. He knew Emily would worry when she found he was missing. But she would come back to look for him in the morning.

Unless Ms. Valentine doesn't let her, he suddenly thought. For a moment, he almost lost his nerve and turned back.

But he couldn't stop. His mind was made up. He had a mission.

He was going to free the ravens.

Chapter Seven
Ravens at Night

Sebastian hurried into the darkness. He hoped Emily wouldn't get in trouble for losing him.

The Tower grounds were spooky, especially for a little bear who wasn't used to being out alone at night. Sebastian's paws were silent on the cobblestone walkway. The only sound was the rustling of leaves.

The farther he went, the darker and spookier it got. Sebastian shivered, remembering Thor's words about ghosts. If there were any, this is when they'd be wandering about.

However, ghosts weren't Sebastian's only

worry. He didn't know where to find the ravens. "I should have asked Thor where he sleeps," he said softly. The sound of his own voice was comforting.

Sebastian decided he'd better start looking for the birds. He climbed on a bench to peek into a narrow window. Pale moonlight reflected off something. Startled, Sebastian almost tumbled backward. At the last minute, he saved himself by grabbing the windowsill.

"It's only armor," he whispered. "Nothing scary." He stayed at the window for several minutes, trying to see inside. *I wish we had gone into this building*, he thought. *It looks interesting.*

For the next half hour, Sebastian peered into window after window. There was no sign of sleeping ravens. Had he gotten himself locked up in the Tower for nothing?

Then he heard something—a dull, clanging sound. A ghost!

Sebastian pressed against a building, hoping his dark fur would hide him. There was no more clanging. But he could hear a soft swish-swish. Did ghosts make swishing noises?

A moment later, a cat came into sight.

Sebastian let out a sigh of relief. At the sound, the cat arched its back. It turned yellow-green eyes in Sebastian's direction.

"It's just me," Sebastian said softly, "Sebastian, a bear." Then he realized that might not be the best thing to say. "A stuffed bear," he added.

"I know that," said the cat. "I can see in the dark. Now, come down here."

Sebastian climbed off the bench and stood in front of the cat. She looked him up and down slowly, then said, "I'm Elizabeth. Named for the queen, you know."

"Oh," said Sebastian "Do you belong to the queen?"

"Goodness, no. I don't belong to anyone. I'm free. I come and go wherever I want. Tonight I want to be here. Now, what are you doing? I've never seen a bear–stuffed or otherwise–wandering the grounds before."

"I'm here because . . . because . . ."

"Come, come. Tell me," said the cat impatiently.

She knows about freedom, thought Sebastian. *Surely she'll understand my mission.* "I'm here to

free the ravens," he said.

"What?"

"They're prisoners," Sebastian explained. "They should be free."

"They've always been here," said Elizabeth. "They wouldn't know what to do out in the world. They're spoiled."

"But shouldn't they be free? Like you and I are?"

"Are you?" Elizabeth asked. "You look like you belong to someone. Someone who takes care of you."

Sebastian ran a paw over his neat clothing. He was free, wasn't he?

When he didn't answer, Elizabeth continued. "Since you're here, you may as well talk to the ravens about the matter. I'll take you to them."

Suddenly, Sebastian had an awful thought. Didn't cats eat birds? The little bear cleared his throat nervously. "Just point me in the right direction," he said. "I don't want to trouble you."

"It's no trouble."

But when Elizabeth walked off, Sebastian didn't follow. The cat looked back over one shoulder. "Are you coming?"

"I . . . I don't think you should come with me. I mean—the ravens are birds. And you're—you're a cat."

Elizabeth's tail twitched angrily. Her eyes flashed. "Do you think I'd eat them? Rubbish! I'm a loyal subject of England. I wouldn't harm a feather on their heads!"

At Sebastian's puzzled look, Elizabeth sighed. "I say, don't you know the legend?"

"Legend?" echoed Sebastian. Then he remembered hearing one of the Yeoman Warders talking about a legend. "I guess I wasn't paying attention," he admitted. "What's the legend?"

"If the ravens leave, the White Tower will crumble. Disaster will come to England."

"Oh," said Sebastian. "Is it true?"

"It must be," said Elizabeth. "The only time there were no ravens here, England was almost invaded."

Sebastian's face fell.

Elizabeth looked at him, then said, "The birds would enjoy a nighttime visitor. Especially one from America. So, come along."

"How did you know I was from America?" Sebastian asked as he followed.

"By the way you talk," said Elizabeth.

Soon they reached the ravens' nesting boxes. Elizabeth meowed three times. A pair of bright eyes peered out from one box.

"Odin," Elizabeth called. "I've brought company. A bear from America."

"I say, that's nice," said Odin. He cawed loudly, and five other heads peeked out. The six ravens fluttered over to where Elizabeth and Sebastian were standing.

"Sebastian!" cried Thor. "What are you doing here?"

"He came to free you," Elizabeth explained.

"But don't you want to be free?" Sebastian asked.

"To free us!" said three ravens at once.

"Whatever for?" asked the largest.

Sebastian looked at the ground, feeling foolish.

"Yes," said Elizabeth. "He's upset that you can't fly away."

"It's kind of you to worry," said Odin. "But we like it here."

"Yes," Thor added. "We're the luckiest birds in London. It's rough in the city. A bird has to fight for every meal out there."

"But don't you want to be free?" Sebastian asked.

One of the smaller ravens said, "We get cranky sometimes because we can't fly. But we can go anywhere we want in the Tower. That's enough freedom for us."

Five heads nodded in agreement.

"Just out of curiosity, how were you planning on freeing us?" Thor asked.

Sebastian looked down again. Actually, he hadn't gotten that far, he realized. Unlike Ms. Valentine, he wasn't much for planning.

"No matter," said Thor. "We're happy to see you."

Elizabeth stretched. "Well, I'll be on my way."

"I'd better go, too," said Sebastian.

"Nonsense," said Odin. "Stay and chat with us for a while."

"Yes, do stay," chorused the other birds.

Sebastian was flattered. "All right," he said. He turned to Elizabeth. "Thanks for helping."

"My pleasure," she said. The ravens cawed good-bye as she walked off. Then they gathered around Sebastian.

"Tell us about America," Odin said.

Sebastian told the ravens about his home with the Parkers. He told them about his travels with Emily and Ben and about New York City, which he had visited. Then the ravens shared tale after tale about the Tower and its visitors.

They certainly can chatter, thought Sebastian.

His eyes drooped. It had been a very long day. The ravens were still talking when Sebastian fell asleep.

Chapter Eight
Belonging

Sebastian groaned and put a paw over his eyes. Why was Emily shining a light in his face?

He slowly opened his eyes. The light was the sun. Morning dew sparkled on Sebastian's fur. He wasn't in the guest house with Emily. He was lying on the grass. Where exactly was he?

Suddenly he remembered. He was in the Tower of London. He had fallen asleep near the ravens' nesting boxes.

Sebastian stretched and yawned. *I have to get back to the gate before the Tower opens*, he thought.

But it was too late. He heard heavy footsteps coming his way. "Oh, no!" he moaned.

Thor's head poked out of a nesting box. "What's

wrong?" he asked.

"Someone's coming. I have to get out of here!"

"It's only the Ravenmaster. He won't hurt you."

"But–"

Sebastian fell silent as a Yeoman Warder came into sight. The Ravenmaster didn't see the bear at first. He checked the nesting boxes, saying hello to each raven in turn. He set out some food for the birds. Then he looked down.

"What's this?" he asked. "A toy?" He picked Sebastian up.

"Someone will be missing you, my fellow," he said kindly.

Emily and Ben will be, thought Sebastian.

The Ravenmaster tucked Sebastian under one arm, then walked off.

"Good luck, Sebastian!" cawed Thor.

"Visit us if you're in England again," Odin added.

Sebastian waved a paw in response. Soon the ravens were out of sight.

"I don't understand how a bear got near the nesting boxes," the Ravenmaster said to himself. "The birds like to pick things up. But usually it's small, shiny things. Not a big, fuzzy bear."

I'm not that big, Sebastian thought.

The Ravenmaster pushed open a door. "I'll just leave you here in my office," he said as he placed Sebastian on a chair.

The little bear was very still until the Ravenmaster left. Then he stood up on the chair to look out the window. He was somewhere in the middle of the Tower area, but he wasn't sure where.

Sebastian slipped off the chair and hurried toward the door. He tugged, but it was too heavy for him. He was trapped.

It was a long morning. Sebastian was beginning to think he would never escape. Emily and Ben would leave London–and him.

Then he heard someone at the door. He scurried back to the chair. Who was coming? What was going to happen to him? He closed his eyes and scrunched down.

"Sebastian!" cried a familiar voice.

"He's here!" cried another.

Sebastian's eyes popped open to see Emily's smiling face. She grabbed him from the chair and squeezed so hard that he gasped for breath.

"Oh, Sebastian, of course you're free."

"Oh, Sebastian," Emily whispered, "I was so scared that I wouldn't find you."

"So was I," Sebastian admitted. "I'm sorry I got lost."

"It's okay. As long as I have you back."

Sebastian turned from Emily to Ms. Valentine, who was standing near the door. From the expression on her face, he could tell that she was unhappy.

"Thank you very much," Ms. Valentine was saying to the warder. Then she added, "Well, our morning is ruined, children. I had planned on taking you back to the British Museum to see the armor display. But there isn't enough time before our plane leaves for Egypt."

"I'm sorry," Emily murmured.

"So am I," Ms. Valentine replied. "After all, you are old enough to be responsible for your belongings." She took Ben by the hand, then turned toward the warder.

"Am I a belonging, Emily?" Sebastian asked.

"What do you mean?"

"Well, am I free? Or do I belong to you?"

For a moment, Emily seemed puzzled. Then she

smiled. "Oh, Sebastian, of course you're free. You only belong to me because I love you. And I belong to you for the same reason."

"Oh," said Sebastian. He thought about what Emily had said and felt warm inside.

"Come, children," sighed Ms. Valentine. "I'm not sure what we'll do next."

As they left the office, Sebastian suddenly remembered something he had seen the night before. "Emily," he said, "we can see some armor. There's lots of it here."

"Really?"

When Sebastian nodded, Emily hurried to catch up with Ms. Valentine and the warder. Breathlessly, she asked, "Isn't there armor here?"

"There certainly is, miss," the warder said. "A fine collection."

"May we see it, Ms. Valentine?" Emily asked.

"Well, I suppose so. It's not what I had planned. But, yes, that would be very educational. And I am very impressed, Emily. You must have read the guidebook to know about the armor."

"I'll show you the way," offered the warder. He marched off with Ms. Valentine at his side.

On the way he explained that one display showed how a king had gained weight. As the king got larger, he kept having to have new armor made to fit him. Ms. Valentine listened happily. She loved to learn new things.

Meanwhile, Sebastian whispered to Emily and Ben, sharing his nighttime adventures and the tales the ravens had told him.

After he finished, Sebastian picked a few blades of grass from his jacket. "Will there be time to change clothes before we leave for Egypt?" he asked.

"Why?" Ben asked.

"I think I'd look neater in my blazer and shorts."

Emily grinned and gave Sebastian another squeeze.

Sebastian squeezed back. He liked belonging.

EXPLORING THE TOWER OF LONDON

By Emily Parker

This is the Thames River.

The Tower of London is the oldest palace of its kind in Europe. It's not really a tower, but a collection of about 20 towers with a big tower in the center and smaller towers built into the two surrounding walls.

It was built more than 900 years ago as a fortress to protect England and a place where the king could be kept safe during an invasion. At the very same place, almost 2,000 years ago, another fortress was built by the Roman emperor Claudius. It must be a very good place for a fortress! Perhaps that's because it's right next to the Thames (pronounced Tems) River–the largest and most famous river in England.

What do you think of this: The King who ordered the Tower of London to be built had just invaded England himself!

Question: The Tower of London used to be a:

- *palace*
- *prison*
- *zoo*
- *mint*
- *fortress*
- *museum*

Palace: For hundreds of years, the kings and queens of England used the Tower of London as a place to stay. Some escaped to the Tower when they needed to find safety. Others used it for special occasions or visits.

Prison: During many periods of history, the Tower was used as a jail. In the 1400s, Henry VIII locked up two of his wives as well as hundreds of other people he called "traitors." More recently, enemy spies were kept as prisoners at the Tower during World War I.

Zoo: The Royal Menagerie was housed in the Lion Tower until 1834. Lions, bears, and even elephants lived there.

Mint: The Royal Mint, along with other government offices, was in the Tower of London until it was moved in 1810. A mint is a place where money is made.

Fortress: The Tower's strong, thick walls helped make it a safe place where kings and queens could be protected during battles or invasions.

Museum: The first tourists may have visited the Tower of London in the 1600s! The first guidebook was published in 1841, and today more than 2 million people visit every year! not counting bears!

history of The Tower

Some of it!

1066	William the Conqueror invaded England.
1078	William ordered work to begin on the Tower.
1100	The first prisoner (that we know about) was locked in the Tower!
1190 – 1285	Two walls were built around the central tower, and a moat was added.
1240	King Henry III whitewashed the central tower, which has been called the White Tower ever since.
1252	A white bear and an elephant were the first animals to live in the Royal Menagerie at the Tower.
1381	During the Peasant's Revolt, 14-year-old King Richard II and his family escaped to the Tower.
1533-1547	Henry VIII sent two of his wives and many other people to prison at the Tower of London.
1643	The Tower was seized from the king by rebels in a civil war. They kept it until 1660.
1649	The original crown jewels were melted down, by order of Parliament, to make coins.
★★★ 1776	*The United States began a revolution to become its own country.*
1834	The Royal Menagerie was moved out of the Tower and sent to what eventually became the London Zoo.
1841	The Crown Jewels were rescued from a great fire in the Tower. The first official Tower of London guidebook for tourists was published.
1914-1918	Enemy spies were jailed at the Tower during World War I.
1930s-40s	The Tower moat, empty of water, was used for vegetable gardens during World War II.
Today	Two-and-a-half million people visit the Tower of London each year!

King Henry VIII

Do you know why people used to say, "The sun never sets on the British Empire?" That's because at one time, England (or the United Kingdom) ruled countries all around the globe, so when the sun was setting in one British colony, it was just coming up in another.

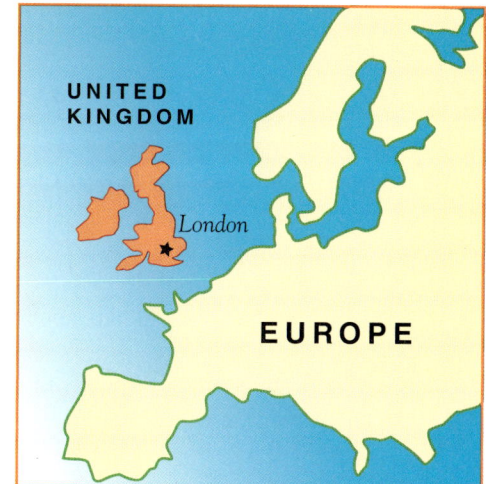

UNITED KINGDOM

London

EUROPE

Sites in London

Trafalgar Square

Picadilly Circus

The Tower of London is in London, England. Did you know that England is not really a country but only part of the *United Kingdom of Great Britain and Northern Ireland*? Most people think of England as a country and think of London as the capital of England. But London is really the capital of the United Kingdom!

Buckingham Palace

The White Tower

Some kings and queens of England used to live here with their families and friends. The walls are as thick as 15 feet! It also housed the first Royal Observatory, where early astronomers studied the stars.

The Crown Jewels

New kings and queens are crowned with the Imperial State Crown. It has 2,868 diamonds, 17 sapphires, 11 emeralds, 5 rubies, and 273 pearls! Other Crown Jewels include one of the largest diamonds in the world (the First Star of Africa), the Black Prince's Ruby and the Stuart Sapphire.

ENTRY TO THE TRAITORS' GATE

Traitor's Gate

This used to be called the Water Gate because it's built over the river. Traitor's Gate is where boats used to enter the Tower hundreds of years ago with prisoners, who were often brought there in secret during the night.

Yeoman Warders

These special guards are only found at the Tower of London. Sometimes called "Beefeaters" no one is sure how they got this nickname. It is a great honor to be a warder; you have to have been in the army for 22 years first! The warders give tours of the Tower to visitors and also live in the Tower with their families.

Did you Know? A special warder called the Yeoman Ravenmaster takes care of the Tower of London ravens.

They wear these red uniforms on special occasions. At other times they wear blue uniforms.

This is a really interesting story!

The Ravens

Hundreds of years ago, there were lots of ravens at the Tower of London. Legend says in the late 1600s, a royal astronomer complained to the king that the ravens were getting in the way of his work. The king wanted to get rid of the birds, but was told that without them the Tower would fall and so would England.

Worried about the legend, the king let some of them stay, and ravens have lived at the Tower ever since. Today, eight ravens live in nesting boxes near Wakefield Tower.

The New Armouries

The Tower of London has one of the best collections of armor in the world. Many of the suits of armor are from the time of Henry VIII (1500s) who actually kept his very own armor at the Tower of London. The king even had a special workshop to make armor especially for him!

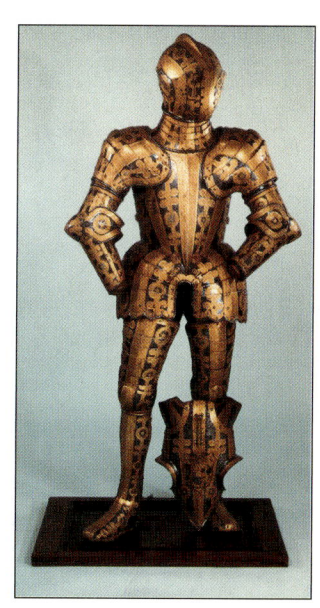

bear&
company™

IF THE POSTCARD below has already been used and you would like a Bear & Company catalog, send your name and address to:

Bear & Company
P.O. Box 3876
Gettysburg, PA 17325

OR visit us on the web at
www.BearandCo.com

OR call 1 800-596-4577

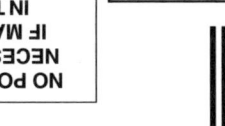

Stories to inspire your imagination . . .
. . . New friends to warm your heart™